First Facts®

Spiders

Barn Spiders

by Molly Kolpin

Consultant:
Pedro Barbosa, PhD
Department of Entomology
University of Maryland, College Park

CAPSTONE PRESS
a capstone imprint

First Facts is published by Capstone Press,
151 Good Counsel Drive, P.O. Box 669, Mankato, Minnesota 56002.
www.capstonepub.com

Books published by Capstone Press are manufactured with paper
containing at least 10 percent post-consumer waste.

Library of Congress Cataloging-in-Publication Data
Kolpin, Molly.
  Barn spiders / Molly Kolpin.
     p. cm.—(First Facts. Spiders)
  Includes bibliographical references and index.
  Summary: "A brief introduction to barn spiders, including their habitat, food, and
life cycle"—Provided by publisher.
  ISBN 978-1-4296-5389-3 (library binding)
  1. Barn spider—Juvenile literature. I. Title.
  QL458.42.A7K65 2011
  595.4′4—dc22
                                                    2010027820

Editorial Credits

Lori Shores, editor; Kyle Grenz, designer; Eric Gohl, media researcher; Laura Manthe,
     production specialist

Photo Credits

Alamy/James Nesterwitz, 12
Fotolia/Kieran Barnes, 1
Pete Carmichael, 21
Photolibrary/Index Stock/Michael Siluk, cover
Shutter Point/Natalja Bindere, 19; Sandra McCabe, 17; Sherry Melville, 15;
Steve Ritzema, 10; Susan Rea, 20
stock.xchng/Cholin, 9
Super Stock Inc./Index Stock, 5, 7

Essential content terms are **bold** and are defined at the bottom of the page
where they first appear.

Printed in the United States of America in Melrose Park, Illinois.

092010   005935LKS11

Table of Contents

Hide and Seek

Hidden against the ground, barn spiders go unseen by **predators**. Their brown and yellow bodies blend into their surroundings. But seen from below, these **arachnids** stand out. Every barn spider has a black mark on its belly. The mark has two white or yellow dots inside it.

predator—an animal that hunts other animals for food
arachnid—an animal with two main body parts, four pairs of legs, and no backbone, wings, or antennae

Itty Bitty Spiders

Barn spiders are less than 1 inch (2.5 centimeters) long. Like all spiders, they have two main body parts and eight legs. Their **abdomens** are large and round. White hairs on their legs help them feel movement.

Spider Fact!

In the book *Charlotte's Web* by E. B. White, Charlotte is a barn spider.

abdomen—the end part of a spider's body

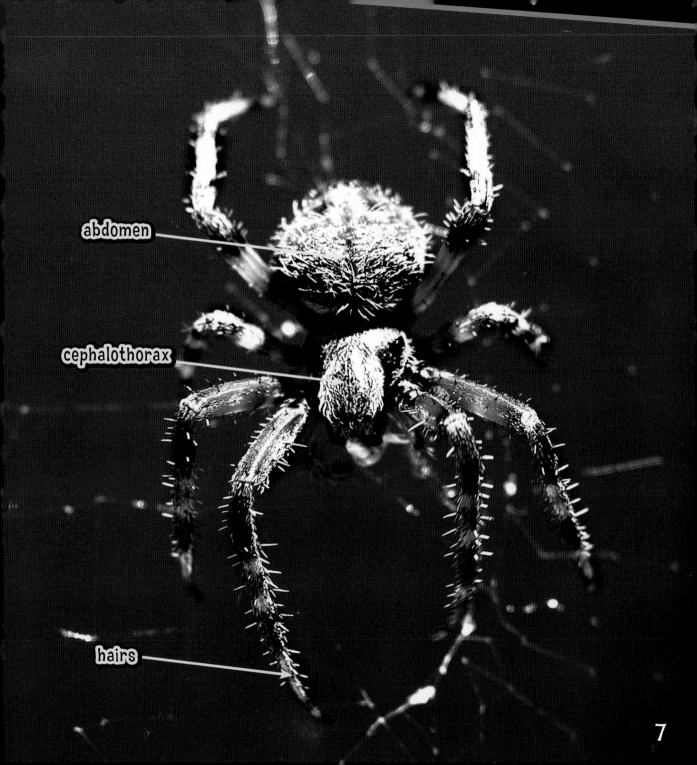

abdomen

cephalothorax

hairs

Country Dwellers

Barn spiders are found only in North America. Many live in Canada and the northeastern United States. But barn spiders have also been seen in the southern United States.

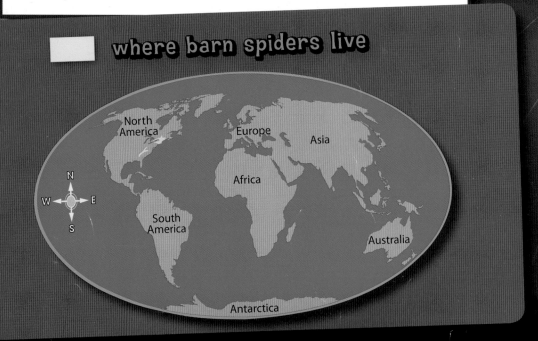

where barn spiders live

Barn spiders earned their name
because they often live in barns. They
also live on porches, bridges, and in
caves. These spiders look for solid
structures on which to build their webs.

Web Masters

Barn spiders are master web builders. Their **orb webs** can be more than 2 feet (0.6 meter) across. It takes them about one hour to make a web from **silk**.

orb web—a round web made of a spiral of silk connected to threads that come out from the center
silk—a string made by spiders

Spider Fact!

Barn spiders sometimes shake their webs back and forth to catch bugs.

Bad News for Bugs

An orb web is a death trap for bugs. Flying bugs become tangled in the sticky silk. As the bugs struggle, they shake the web. The shaking tells the barn spider that it has caught **prey**.

Midnight Meals

Once a bug is trapped, the spider wraps the prey in a piece of the web. **Venom** from the spider's bite quickly kills the prey. The venom also turns the bug into a liquid. Then the spider slurps it up.

Spider Fact!

Because barn spiders use pieces of their webs to wrap prey, the webs become filled with holes.

venom—a harmful liquid that some animals make

Lazy Days

Barn spiders hunt and eat only at night. In the morning, these spiders eat their webs. Then they rest in a hidden spot to stay safe from predators during the day.

17

Baby Barn Spiders

In fall, male and female barn spiders join together to produce young. The female barn spider lays 200 to 500 eggs. She wraps the eggs in an **egg sac**. **Spiderlings** hatch from the eggs in spring.

Spider Fact!

The female spider dies soon after placing the eggs in the egg sac.

egg sac—a small pouch made of silk that holds spider eggs
spiderling—a young spider

Life Cycle of a Barn Spider

Newborn

Spiderlings make webs right after they hatch.

Young

Spiders shed their outer skeletons as they grow.

Adult

Barn spiders live for one year.

Taking Flight

Spiderlings spread out to find new homes by ballooning. Each spider lets out a line of silk and lets the wind carry it away. When the spider lands, it finds a place to build its first web.

Amazing but True!

Barn spiders eat twice their own weight in bugs each day. In just one year, a single barn spider will eat about 2,000 bugs. And that doesn't include bugs it catches but doesn't eat!

Glossary

abdomen (AB-duh-muhn)—the end part of a spider's body

arachnid (uh-RACK-nid)—an animal with four pairs of legs and no backbone, wings, or antennae

egg sac (EG SAK)—a small pouch made of silk that holds spider eggs

orb web (ORB WEB)—a round web made of a spiral of silk connected to threads that come out from the center

predator (PRED-uh-tur)—an animal that hunts other animals for food

prey (PRAY)—an animal hunted by another animal for food

silk (SILK)—a string made by spiders

spiderlings (SPYE-dur-ling)—a young spider

venom (VEN-uhm)—a harmful liquid that some animals make

Read More

Rene, Ellen. *Investigating Spiders and Their Webs.* Science Detectives. New York: PowerKids Press, 2009.

Stewart, Melissa. *How do Spiders Make Webs? Tell Me Why, Tell Me How.* New York: Marshall Cavendish Benchmark, 2009.

Woodward, John. *Spider.* Garden Minibeasts Up Close. New York: Chelsea Clubhouse, 2010.

Internet Sites

FactHound offers a safe, fun way to find Internet sites related to this book. All of the sites on FactHound have been researched by our staff.

Here's all you do:

Visit *www.facthound.com*

Type in this code: 9781429653893

 Check out projects, games and lots more at
www.capstonekids.com

Index